TOWARD THE NEW DEGENERACY

Bruce Benderson

BRUCE BENDERSON

Toward
The New Degeneracy

AN ESSAY

EDGEWISE
New York - Paris - Turin
24 FIFTH AVENUE, N° 224
1997

TOWARD THE NEW DEGENERACY: AN ESSAY
by Bruce Benderson.
Copyright © 1997 Bruce Benderson.
All Rights Reserved.
Published by Edgewise Press, Inc.
New York - Paris - Turin.
Edgewise Press: 24 Fifth Avenue, N° 224, New York, N.Y. 10011.
First Edition, May 1997.
Library of Congress Catalogue Card Number: 96-061925.
I.S.B.N.: 0-96464466-3-3.
Printed by Polo Grafiche Dal Broi & Fracchia srl, Turin, Italy.
Frontispiece photograph of the author by Marion Ettlinger, 1994.
Versions of some of these essays appeared in the magazines
Konkret (Germany); *Cups;* and the World Wide Web magazines
Artnet, *Alt-X*, and *Dent.*
Special thanks to Joy L. Glass & Erika Knerr.

CONTENTS

TOWARD THE NEW DEGENERACY

Degenerates are not always criminals, prostitutes, anarchists, and pronounced lunatics; they are often authors and artists.

Max Nordau, *Degeneration*, 1892

So there was a new breed of adventurers, urban adventurers who drifted out at night looking for action with a black man's code to fit their facts.

Norman Mailer, "The White Negro," 1957

TOWARD THE NEW DEGENERACY

I

What are the compromises of the new witch hunt? This was the question I asked myself in 1979 as I sat editing the "evolution disclaimer." The disclaimer was a stamp to be applied to every sixth grade science book adopted by the state of Texas. It admitted that the textbook discussed Darwin's theories of evolution but denied that this was in any way an annulment of the theory of Adam and Eve.

Such an addition to the book promised to be Midas's touch. Winning the approval of the Texas school system meant seven-figure profits for the publisher. Every copy of the book sent to Texas could be stamped, but the disclaimer did not have to appear on shipments going to the more liberal states. Complicating this bizarre commercial and ideological enterprise even more was the actual text inside the book. For over four months I'd carefully edited the manuscript, obeying a specially prepared list of nonracist, nonsexist words that now made some passages read like a software-run translation from another language. In fact, three entire units used only plural pronouns because the nonsexist pronoun group "he or she" would lengthen sentences and drive up the "reading level."

How had these two absurd agendas from the Right and from the Left — one blurring claims about human prehistory from apes and the other softening descriptive language about living humans — come together? Years later I would cease to wonder. My textbook, which also had a chapter on the reproductive system, but no "he's" or "she's," was the precursor of a new conspiracy between two former enemies. Each had its grievances against the other, yet each agreed about the need to promote certain community standards.

Today we live the full flowering of that centrist paradise. Though few admit it, textbooks that simultaneously satisfy creationist beliefs and avoid sexist language are the "one-size-fits-all" of a very specific class. One main objective of these books is not to inform but to soothe tensions of difference and create the illusion of community. But the basic atoms of the structure of this community are the nuclear family, an element proven to be highly unstable. The fact that the family is now seen by everyone as the building block of the social order is why even the Left sees no psychoanalytic irony in gay lib tee-shirts reading, "Hate Is Not a Family Value." Neither Left nor Right can admit how hate and resentment keep the nuclear family's incestuous urges tensely leashed. No one points to the many instances in which the goals of family and community are set against other members of society.

Twenty-seven years ago nobody could have convinced me that any particular class could covertly form a strong coalition in America, or that the agendas of the Left and the Right could ever be confounded with each other in the promotion of a single monotonous style of community life. At the time, I sleep-walked through a counterculture existence on public welfare in the hippie Haight Ashbery. My life was one of glaring contradictions. I would purify my blood with macrobiotics and ginseng root but poison it with hallucinogenic toxins and frequent bouts of gonorrhea. Because I was void of ambition and virtually without contact with the conventional workaday world, I thought that world was practically extinct. But my disdain for the material comforts of middle class life never encroached upon my unending hunger for instant gratification. And I never understood how similar my impulses were to those of other consumers.

How could I have guessed that my sexual freedom would become shrouded by condom-consciousness? How would I have known that my hippie friends' nostalgia for rural space would mutate into the activism of the block association and its sullen war against street people? Who would have dared to suggest that the fight for sexual rights could come to include a crusade against sexual abuse partly relying upon Victorian ideals of child protection? Or that violent campus uprisings would give birth to grievance committees that haggled over the crimes of politically incorrect speech? I didn't; but perhaps it was because I had never considered the class context in which the supposedly seismic changes of the sixties occurred.

My counterculture movement was a half-child of the Beat phenomenon that came before it and was thwarted. What made this phenomenon a foregone conclusion just a decade later was its profound connection to the city — just at the time when the next generation was being inculcated with the values of suburban life. Hipsters were attracted to the black jazz and intravenous drug subcultures of cities. They themselves came mostly from backgrounds that had little to do with these urban elements. Their niche was small and unstable. It was hostile to the middle class, but it was alienated from the working class due to the failures of thirties socialism.

In *Down and In: Life in the Underground*, Ronald Sukenick describes the Beats' early colonization of Greenwich Village, under the disapproving gaze of the neighborhood's Italian working class toughs. No one who faced the grim reality of low income but who had hopes of improving his condition saw anything romantic about forfeiting opportunities for education or employment. To find soulmates, the hipsters took a detour around the working class in search of those whose goals were short-term, pleasure-oriented, and anti-work.

In 1957 Norman Mailer wrote his notorious definition of the hipster in an essay called "The White Negro." The piece was a follow-up to a provocative statement he had sent to journalists and leading writers such as William Faulkner, suggesting that what Southern whites most feared about the black man was his sexual potency. "The White Negro" was a corollary of this proposition. It boasted that the hip white nonconformist was a voluntary "psychopath," whose attitudes and life style mirrored those of the alienated American black. This idea was almost as repugnant when Mailer suggested it as it is by today's politically correct standards. In the black man, Mailer had attempted to locate all that was libidinal, rebellious, spontaneous, amoral, and infantile: all the impulses that make self-gratification the highest priority of the creative person and delayed gratification the province of the Square. Because these libidinal energies seemed so at odds with the current values of the decade in which Mailer was writing, he spoke of them using the sensationalized and morbid term "psychopath." Little did he know that just a decade later, the same loose id would be recast as a state of "higher consciousness" and instant gratification would be lauded as a "groovy" pursuit.

Mailer's use of the term "psychopath" was, in actuality, deliberately obnoxious. It was an attention-getting tactic for a world view that was more than willfully amoral. Being a "White Negro" meant accepting "the terms of death" and living with "death as immediate danger" at the dawning of the age of the atom bomb. It was a consciousness that urged one "to explore that domain of experience where security is boredom and therefore sickness," an attitude that so jarred with the optimistic tone of the times that it forced the "bohemian and the juvenile delinquent [to come] face-to-face with the Negro, and [made] the hipster a fact in American life."

The dropouts of the sixties who flocked to San Francisco may have been inspired by the hip "psychopaths" of the fifties, but they were curiously non-urban and very picky about the aspects of the down-and-out life to which they were willing to relate. They came mostly from middle class white suburban homes and isolated nuclear families. They did not, as a rule, mix with the leather-jacketed working class juvenile delinquents who were the other alienated youths of their time. The hippies wanted their lives to be a sensory bath that would make up for the monotony of the suburbs without sacrificing some of its conveniences, but their vision of the sensory was a living-color spectacle inspired by television and film. Perhaps the aspect of Beat culture that most inspired their split-level minds was the landscape of the open highway, promoted by Kerouac.

Unlike the Beats, whose philosophical tone was colored by European cafe existentialism and by the old dichotomy between the avant-garde and the bourgeoisie, the hippies of the sixties felt that heavy intellectualizing hampered creative and spontaneous behavior and that art sprang from the popular culture that they already liked. Their underground found its easiest outlets for spontaneity and pleasure in things that had mass appeal. This led to a self-destructing alliance with the mainstream. "During the sixties and seventies," writes Sukenick in *Down and In*, "the middle class and the counterculture fell into a complicitous pseudopopulism, which in any case is the main phony mode of American politics. The major message of pseudopopulism seems to be that what is good for the middle class is good for the people, while the needs of actual people, middle class or otherwise, are ignored in the name of populism." The "main phony mode" would also become a major field for commentary for avant-garde artists, as typified by Warhol's cynical embrace of pop. Sukenick feels, at any rate, that complicity with the middle class is the fate of any American vanguard movement, since the middle class claims to be only a "situation incidental to capitalist economics" and is willing to absorb any culture of profit potential that comes along.

The shift away from heroin toward psychedelics during the sixties also worked to cleanse the underground of its links to the ghetto and to crime. Mailer's extended simile of the White Negro was offensive to the new generation. In the first place, they found it glaringly racist to locate any particular set of qualities at all within a particular race. And to flower children it seemed perverse, as well, to suggest that a life devoted to pleasure could be nothing but destructive and dark. What is more, they weren't as pessimistic as the Beats, who had implicitly assumed that they could not easily succeed in upsetting and reshaping social norms. What wasn't apparent at the time was that the vibrant new culture of the sixties was politically ineffectual, because it was unconsciously interested in middle class opportunities. It was a consumer subculture, boasting greatly original personal styles, but with little power to change the monolithic institutions of America.

Within the decadent playpen of the sixties mind, some of the West's most eccentric personal quests were carried out. New frontiers of sexual identity, ancient pagan rituals, Eastern approaches to death, and new uses of drugs flourished like outlandish weeds. Genius became a perfection of life style and was decidedly non-literary. Art ceased to be isolated from the artist's sexual tastes, personal fantasies, clothing, or interest in drugs; and the cult of personality took on crucial importance. The movement grew to include a larger and larger segment of the middle class, until suddenly even the most radical dropouts found that they were no longer in a meaningful adversarial position. They were safely included in the American economy and American mind.

In those naive days I still saw my life style as a potent revolt against the monogamous sexual couple, the dynamics of the nuclear family, and the working world. What I didn't realize at the time was that the random couplings I so enjoyed could sometimes result in a real dyad — be it heterosexual or homosexual, with all its conventional aspirations of fidelity, family dynamics, and isolation from the Other; that my idealization of spontaneous "childlikeness" was an acceptance of the cult of the child, invented for the Victorian family and rife with covert strategies for diminishing the power and danger of childhood energies; or that my impulsiveness could be harnessed to consumerism. What I also didn't realize is that the alternative existence I sought had already been described and condemned several times by bourgeois spokesmen in the war against degeneration.

In 1892, Max Nordau, a Jewish Hungarian journalist living in Paris, began a strangely personalized war against that era's counterculture life styles. In a book entitled *Degeneration*, he launched an attack upon the Symbolists and those who in the future would be known as Expressionists, whose mentality he claimed was irrational, pessimistic, impulsive, darkly naturalistic, subversive, mannered, unresolved, solipsistic, experimental, and hyper-aesthetic. To combat these degenerates, Nordau stressed simplicity, classical art forms, clear-headedness, materialism, physical culture, strength of will, the natural sciences, and bourgeois morality. In other words, Nordau single-handedly tried to keep the revolution of Modernist sensibility from happening.

Today the rhetoric of Nordau's claims seems preposterous and obscene, because they rely heavily upon biological factors as the cause of most unconventional behavior; but his writings were taken seriously and even highly acclaimed until the First World War, after which it became apparent that the aesthetic styles and philosophical stances against which he railed were to forge the basic tenets of twentieth century avant-garde thought. Also, Freud's theories had begun to shed ridicule on the old ideas about a correlating physical cause for all mental problems. By the 1920s this once famous critic had sunk into complete obscurity. Yet today we find many of the attitudes in Nordau's middle class doctrine echoed in the new emphasis on organic causes of mental disorders as diverse as schizophrenia and depression, on clean living through diet and exercise, on accessible art for the masses, and on the pre-eminence of family values.

Nordau's claims are cast in a Darwinian framework such as would be absurd and repulsive today. He believed that the abnormal behavior of the degenerate was the product of a biologically inferior or organically damaged mind that could even be recognized in certain subtle body deformities, but that the process of natural selection would weed out degeneracy over the course of generations. He also used evolution as a rationale for opposing political revolution, claiming that since evolutionary change is gradual and needs no outside interference, governments will change naturally over time.

Nordau's philosophy was one of bourgeois sagacity rooted in biological purity. In a way it was diametrically opposed to everything that Mailer would later idealize in the White Negro. Nordau's cause was taken up at various times by doctors, critics, and the French Communist party, all of whom, until World War I, saw him as an eminent crusader for progress and a champion in the war against decadence and regressive behavior. This was, at the time, a typically *liberal* point of view, for what distinguished liberalism then, and what ties it to its present incarnation, is its class sensibility. Although the middle class liberals of today may pride themselves on a certain open-mindedness, they also believe in the main tenets of their class, which include rationality, will-power, discipline, and social and scientific progress. It is contemporary liberalism's emphasis on the nuclear family as the root of everything that is good that seems to be moving it closest to that provincial liberalism of the late nineteenth century, in which the goodness of the drawing room was thought to be inviolable.

Nordau's basic causes for degeneration of body and mind were eerily similar to those touted by today's anti-tobacco activists, self-help groups, natural food advocates, and ecology activists. He said that degeneration was caused by a poisoning of the body through the use of alcohol, tobacco, narcotics, and stimulants; as well as the stress of city living and the toxins of industry. He thought these health hazards decayed the brain, leading to many perversions, including the preference for the aesthetic over the useful. He maintained, for example, that the pointillism of contemporary painters was caused by overexcited nerve vibrations, and that the pessimism of the Naturalists was caused by the enervations of city living.

What these theories boiled down to, finally, was that all of the sober standards of middle class life were essential to the very survival of the species. In such a scheme, Mailer's White Negro would have been branded as Public Enemy No. 1. Nordau thought art was O.K., as long as it served the middle class community and could be understood by its most average members. It had to recycle time-honored classical forms and emphasize action, plot, and the moral message. Along this line, he became an early proponent of popism, maintaining that an entertainment that appealed to the common man had to be for the good of the community. His politically correct art form was today's "G" film with the happy ending.

In more than 500 pages Nordau belligerently described all of the characteristics of degeneration, proving, he thought, how it issued from minds organically debased by inferior inheritance and bad habits and demonstrating how degeneration poisoned the majority of artistic creations and design styles of his era. The beginning of the book set forth the symptoms, diagnosis, and etiology of the social disease that had infected culture. The last two chapters offered a prognosis and therapeutics for the cure.

The symptoms of the disease included overaffected clothing fashions, dandyish mannerisms, baroque fin-de-siècle salon interiors, Wagnerian chromatics, and Zolaesque wallowing in urban filth. All these were catalogued by Nordau in a manner worthy of the decadent novel *A rebours* by Huysmans, an author who is one of the many pre-Modernists lambasted in Nordau's book. Nordau's diagnosis of the social illness of degeneration is also a condemnation of the "purely literary mind, whose merely aesthetic culture does not enable him to understand the connections of things, and to seize their real meaning..." The "connections of things" were something that could only be thoroughly understood by scientists

Mannered aesthetes, mystics, Symbolists, Decadents, Diabolists, Ibsenists, and Wagnerians were the White Negroes of Nordau's day. They suffered, according to him, not only from a kind of hysteria that often satisfies itself in verbal outpourings, but in certain physical markers of degeneration. Nordau borrowed this idea from noted biological determinists of his day and earlier, such as Franz Joseph Gall and Caesar Lombroso, to whom the book is dedicated. He reasoned that if he were given the opportunity to examine those suspected of moral degeneration, he would undoubtedly discover corresponding physical deformities. But the demands of privacy made this impossible, and it was not, in fact, called for, since, "It is not necessary to measure the cranium of an author or to see the lobe of a painter's ear, in order to recognize the fact that he belongs to the class of degenerates."

If a degenerate became a novelist, reasoned Nordau, his narrator would be likely to confound right and wrong. Nordau had witnessed the avant-garde intellectuals of his day going to great lengths to show the relativity of questions of good and evil. He did not think such degenerates were blatant criminals, but he accused them of the nearly criminal act of trying to prove the "theoretical legitimacy of crime." They were borderline cases who should have known better, like Mailer's White Negroes. They "discover beauties in the lowest and most repulsive things."

Like Mailer's White Negroes, they were characterized by an "unbounded egoism" and "impulsiveness," stigmatized by "emotionalism" and "pessimism," and disinclined to positive action. In fact, it was likely that many were disciples of Schopenhauer or practiced Buddhism. Add to this taste for mysticism a predilection for flights of the imagination, an impressionable nature, and even "an irresistible desire...to accumulate useless trifles," a sickness Nordau dubbed the "buying craze," borrowing a term from the psychologist Magnan.

As has been mentioned, Nordau traced the etiology of the cultural disease of degeneration partly to poisoning through drug addiction, an attitude strangely prophetic of today's proponents of the war on drugs, who love to attribute our major social ills to the problem of urban drug abuse with little reference to the vicissitudes of class and poverty or social or psychological conditioning. However, Nordau added a pre-Fascist biological imperative to his etiology, writing that, "A race which is regularly addicted to narcotics and stimulants in any form (such as fermented alcoholic drinks, tobacco, opium, hashish, arsenic), which partakes of tainted foods (bread made with bad corn), which absorbs organic poisons (marsh fever, syphilis, tuberculosis, goitre), begets degenerate descendants who, if they remain exposed to the same influences, rapidly descend to the lowest degrees of degeneracy, to idiocy, to dwarfishness, etc."

To all the causes of degeneracy, Nordau added one other crucial influence: residence in large towns, pointing out that, "Parallel with the growth of large towns is the increase in the number of the degenerate of all kinds

— criminals, lunatics...; and it is natural that these last should play an ever more prominent part in endeavoring to introduce an ever greater element of insanity into art and literature."

His alliance with the wholesome would backfire, of course. For though his insistence upon clean living and scientific thought jived with the values of the bourgeoisie, his theories about the link between physical and psychological degeneration would feed the Nazi's racial theories about Jews, of which Nordau was one. He died in 1923, without seeing the Holocaust, but not before it was hinted to his disadvantage that viciousness, degenerate tastes, and moral aberrations can fester and grow within a context of family values and physical purity. Still, one cannot stress how much his supposedly outmoded world view resembles the one currently in vogue among today's centrist social critics in our media and government. These modern hygienists deplore the decay of the city, the corrosion of drugs, and the hazards of pollution as if they were evil entities independent of other conditions. They hold them up to middle class models of mental, physical, and sexual health. They call for an end to urban crime but do not want to delve into the connected complexities of class or money. And they use the controlling cultural institutions of the suburban life style as basic assumptions, similar to the way in which Nordau equated science with the rituals of the Victorian drawing room.

What Nordau, today's journalists and politicians, and to some extent, Norman Mailer left out of their for-

mulas about marginality was conceptualized in a radical
way by one social scientist widely read during the 1950s
and 1960s. His name was Oscar Lewis and he is today
almost as out of vogue as Nordau became. In 1965, at
the time of the war on poverty, Lewis published *La
Vida: A Puerto Rican Family in the Culture of Poverty
— San Juan and New York*, a study based on Puerto
Rican families from two slums of San Juan and their rel-
atives in New York City. In this book and others, Lewis
was bold enough to advance the theory of a universal
culture of poverty, given the right economic and political
conditions. His definition of the culture of poverty was
based on 80 characteristics that he thought could be discovered in the slums of any modern nation, regardless of
climate, race, or cultural heritage of those involved.
Many of the individual psychological traits Lewis lists
are characteristic of Mailer's glorified Negro, but Lewis
took care to point out that "many of the problems we
think of as distinctively our own or distinctively Negro
problems (or that of any other special racial or ethnic
group) also exist in countries where there are no distinct
ethnic minority groups."

Lewis's 80 characteristics also match many of
Nordau's symptoms of degeneration. When one consid-
ers that Nordau's interest in degeneration was mostly a
way of refuting the spontaneity, alienation, or pessimism
of the avant-garde artists of the time, and that Mailer's
White Negro was a way of restoring these qualities to
white artists by encouraging them to emulate the urban
black, a spiritual coalition between the culture of poverty
and the culture of bohemia is revealed.

However, Lewis's position is seen today by many as a prejudicial indictment of the poor, with racist and classist overtones. The effrontery of assigning a cultural identity with psychological traits to a segment of the population caught in economic deprivation is interpreted as snobbism, as if one were saying: "We all know what *those* people are like." There is today an unspoken agreement among people of the mainstream media to pretend that everyone shares the same (middle class) values and that some — either because of or in spite of individual character — are (temporarily) caught in unpleasant situations or have become inexplicably evil. If a woman in a housing project who smokes crack leaves her three-year-old child to starve for several days, the report on the evening news implies that she is different from us only in regard to this isolated action. It is as if a familiar middle class persona were magically converted from Jekyll to Hyde, an event explainable in the terminology of drug abuse or crime but never in a cultural context that includes the values or economic variables of the perpetrator's community. Lewis was bold enough to suggest that economics and political control could create a lasting, uniform, inherited culture *that was even more powerful than an inherited ethnicity* and that this culture was a context in which these events so unusual to us took place. Nor did Lewis wish to romanticize or indict the poor, but merely to demonstrate that their culture was "an effort to cope with feelings of hopelessness and despair which develop from the realization of the improbability of achieving success in terms of the values and goals of the larger society." He also appreciated

some of the positive aspects of the culture of poverty —
the sensuality, spontaneity, sense of adventure, and
indulgence of impulses that come from living in the present time. "Perhaps it is this reality of the moment which
the existentialist writers are so desperately trying to
recapture but which the culture of poverty experiences as
natural, everyday phenomena," he went so far as to say,
linking the metaphysics of the culture of poverty to those
of the Modernist and the hipster.

Like Mailer's Negroes and White Negroes, and
Nordau's degenerates, members of the culture of poverty
are contemptuous of the dominant institutions of middle
class life. They hate the police, mistrust government
officials, and even feel a cynicism about the church.
They are aware of middle class values and may even
espouse them, but do not live by them. Their communities lurch along with a minimum of planning and organi-
zation, and individuals are apt to go where the day takes
them. They have debunked the Victorian ideal of childhood as a state of protracted innocence by shortening the
period of protection to which a child is entitled.
Although they may claim strong family values, mar-
riages tend to be consensual rather than legal, there is a
high incidence of abandonment, and sibling rivalry is a
constant threat to nuclear family functioning.

Sex fills a diverse set of needs for the members of
the culture of poverty and encompasses pleasure, money,
love, and machismo achievement. The incest taboo is
less rigid in family life, and male children are sometimes
erotically stimulated by mothers and other family members to develop pride in their erections. Nordau would

not approve of such a family setting, but he would be
more likely to link such behavior to biological inheritance or "poisoning" than to poverty. Mailer would
approve, but he would find his causes in the sociology of
race in America.

When reading Lewis, one must come to the conclusion that in respect to the poor's libidinal mentality, they
are like bohemians. They "show a great zest for life,
especially for sex, and a need for excitement, new experiences and adventures.... They value acting out more
than thinking out, self-expression more than self-con-
straint, pleasure more than productivity, spending more
than saving, personal loyalty more than impersonal jus-
tice." Certainly these qualities were familiar to anyone in
fin-de-siècle Paris, in Beat San Francisco, or throughout
the sprawling sixties underground.

The geographical interfacing of the culture of poverty and the "willfully poor" bohemian is familiar to us
today in urban neighborhoods such as New York's East
Village. Communities like the East Village begin when
young, alienated newcomers arrive to superimpose a
quirky and extemporaneous culture upon a traditionally
immigrant neighborhood. Although the neighborhood
will still be largely populated by the very poor (those too
poor to object), the ones who come to take advantage of
the situation are largely from middle class, working
class, or upper class backgrounds and are mostly white
and often artistically inclined. Some are self-styled anarchists, and many are vociferously alienated from the
American mainstream. They come not only in search of

cheap rents, but because aspects of the culture of poverty suit their makeshift professional style, their chaotic schedules, and the openness of their sex lives. But even though the atmosphere of abject poverty facilitates the life of bohemia, there is very little mixing with it.

The locals respond with varying degrees of hostility to the greenhorns who come to create an underground, just as the Italian working class hoods described in Sukenick's *Down and In* gave the evil eye to West Village interlopers in 1948. The newcomers may emulate the fashions of the culture of poverty from a distance and certainly draw a charge from its noisy and chaotic energy on the street; but once bohemia takes root in a neighborhood, many of those who promoted it, who always had other options, and who are unconsciously inculcated with the middle class values of their past, suddenly find themselves with changed allegiances. They change the terrain as they change, instituting block associations, co-ops, community police groups, and private day care centers to combat the very instabilities that once attracted them.

This does not explain, however, why today's underground has produced less of an avant-garde — in literature, art, or fashion — than the late nineteenth century European culture of the cafes, which germinated Modernism; the Beats, who christened a new school of American literature and interfaced with the Abstract Expressionists; or the hippies, whose rapport with mass culture shaped the entertainment and sexual mores of the seventies. The reason bohemia has lost its teeth today is because its energy source — its vital links with the culture of poverty — have been all but severed. The dulling of the counterculture edge began when the spontaneity, sexual promiscuity, and pop tastes of the hippies found too little a likeness in the energies of rejected people. This attitude developed by the eighties into the opportunistic alienation of the yuppies.

In fact, the very *disorganization* of the culture of poverty, which is the key both to its spontaneity and its quirky energy, frightened the hippies and the next generation of suburban exiles. Many came from homes where corporations and civic institutions weren't mystifying faraway cabals. Their need for order, lasting self-gratification, and security was bound to rear its head. The symptoms in their split allegiances were there from the start in their linguistic style. They had a suburban fear of the exaggeration, boasting, and macho obfuscation of underclass communication. They never developed their own complete argot. Although hippie language did have its slang, this never differentiated much from the suburban language of the Valley Girl. Conversely, if one looks back another decade, it becomes clear that there was a time when Beat argot was so infused with the rhythms of jazz that it could barely be understood by outsiders. All the subversive values of the Hip culture were encoded within it. The White Negro enjoyed a special link to urban ghetto culture, which kept him marginal but vital.

II

I grew up as the son of a lawyer in Syracuse, New York, a suburban-style city with a population so median that it is a center for market research testing of new products. When I came to New York's East Village in 1974, after four and a half years in San Francisco, I did not understand that my counterculture ideology wouldn't be enough to keep me from plunging into an identity crisis. My socially ambiguous existence as a marginal would gradually come to seem flaccid and ineffectual. This was perplexing to me because, on the surface, my pleasure-oriented activities had seemed a subversive dumping of my middle class past.

For the last four and a half years I'd taken homosexual experiments to extremes. Several nights a week in the baths and back rooms of San Francisco had brought the total number of different sex partners into the thousands. Though I'd been writing fiction, I was unpublished and working in a narcissistic vacuum. Up to that moment I had adamantly refused to use my liberal arts education for any occupation or mode of communication that felt "professional."

There was something anticlimactic about the permissive climate of the mid-seventies, a hollow feeling about the libidinal prizes for which we had strived in the preceding decade. At the beginning, I'd been attracted by the new identity politics forming around sexual orientation. This came from the fact that I'd been galvanized as a teenager by John Rechy's *City of Night* and Burrough's *Junky* and was convinced that the political power of homosexuality lay in its implicit subversion of the daily life of the family. In 1969, in San Francisco and Berkeley, I'd joined the gay liberation movement and, appearing with matted hair and ripped jeans, helped picket homophobic radio stations, stage fuck-ins on church banquettes, and invade a convention of the American Psychiatric Association that was exhibiting an electrode shock machine used to convert homosexuals by aversion therapy.

Back then, I was under the quaint and happy impression that the homosexual was a powerful taunt to society's dearest assumptions. I was heartened by what I thought was homosexual privilege — the fact that our group defied the biological laws of succession and were thus the only group that could not be permanently eliminated. You could kill me, but not what I stood for, because my people didn't need gay mothers or fathers to be reborn. On the other hand, when genocidal Spaniards killed off all the Taino's on the island of Puerto Rico, they disappeared from the planet. When the Polish and German Jews were exterminated, no one could ever replace their numbers. As a group, homosexuals were luckier. They could never be eliminated for more than a generation after which they would return again as the children of unwitting heterosexuals to mock the tyranny of procreation.

I also highly valued the experiential vigor of homosexual promiscuity. In a world in which middle class people were increasingly shutting out other classes, the willingness to fuck opened class and age barriers. The gay world was a place where the retired doctor might adopt the street boy hustler or the Harvard student could find himself in bed with a forty-year-old mechanic. My sexual escapades had made me privy to life styles, class realties, and ethnicities most people of my background never encountered.

Why, then, this feeling of irrelevancy as the years of the 1970s rolled by? Perhaps it was a foreshadowing of the limitations of identity politics. It would become apparent — a decade later — that a politics concerned with who you are is the politics of a particular class and that all it can offer to assimilated minorities — be they black, female, or gay — is a holding cell that serves to define them as a particular subculture of that class.

As the 70s progressed, identity politics would not only become the only politics of the Left, but it would be shaped by minorities within the educated classes, whose need for assimilation would recast subversive elements of society — homosexuals, ghetto inhabitants, or alcoholics — as normal people who participated at least mentally in wholesome middle class life and were in need of protection and help. This was the legacy of the new "suburbanized" counterculture. John Rechy's homosexuals and Hubert Selby, Jr.'s addicts had found solidarity among other addicts, transvestites, prostitutes, and petty criminals. Those shaped by identity politics would seek the approval of politicians, family members, corporations, and the clergy.

In the universities, identity politics turned the feisty, rageful dialectic of the Outsider into a polite multicultural tea party. It eventually drained discussions of race,

gender, and sexual orientation of irony and opportunities
for humor because its rhetoric came from one protected
cultural class. Lenny Bruce had understood the power of
the epithet and its great opportunities for irony and paro-
dy. University grievance committees do not. Politically
correct terms became a way of keeping difference at a
respectful distance that amounts to denial, and labeling
began to embalm what it described. Euphemisms like
"people of color" sounded like "Mr." to me, who remem-
bered a recent time when people had grown used to call-
ing each other by their first names. The severing of the
old, unspoken intimacy between the bohemian, the ghetto
dweller, and the radical, which had started with the hippies, was completed by this new politics. Gay libera-
tionists and feminists redefined the troublesome underclass, who reappeared only as bashers, batterers, sex
objects who did not understand their oppression, victims,
or macho closet cases.

In formulating the new emphasis on identity and
assimilation, the middle classes unwittingly conspired to
strangle libido and lower class expression. But I didn't
understand this yet. Thinking of myself as a liberated
homosexual, I continued to comb through the liberal gay
papers, occasionally wondering why the articles on culture seemed so repetitive. To avoid stereotyping, the journalists had self-censored most of the generalizations
needed to talk about groups. One had to vehemently deny
that gays were abnormal or different from anyone else,
but one also had to insist on the necessity of our own
books, magazines, and clubs. As these writers fumbled to
locate a shared gay identity, they nervously tiptoed past

any controversial pronouncements about gays. The result-
ing cultural discussion was bland, a concentration on
fashion styles and modes of humor among homosexuals.

Malaise overtook me in the late seventies. I wanted
to escape for even a moment from the pressures of my
self-imposed identity, as well as my class, my family,
the world. I found that escape momentarily in pornogra-
phy, which today is the last allowable transgressive
expression of bourgeois consciousness. For a few
moments leading to orgasm, it was possible to evade
Nordau's wholesome world of anti-urban family wis-
dom, plain-spoken honesty, and non-fragmentary plots, a
world which had expanded horrifyingly in contemporary
times to co-opt its old enemies — removing some of the
stigma Nordau placed on homosexuality, mental illness,
or addiction in order to suck these marginals into a dena-
tured pocket of the bourgeoisie. The senseless, unreal
prolongations of sexual energy on the video screen or in
grimy porno theaters eclipsed worries about family protection and budget management. The amoral bath of las-
civiousness suspended for a moment the march of
progress. This mass-produced clinically revealed sex
mocked Nordau's equation of science, reason, and bourgeois moderation, which was about to become again so
popular as we neared the end of this century.

Then came the sledge hammer. AIDS simultaneously ruined my momentary escapes from a decent curtailed
identity and smashed the idea I had of promiscuity as an
effortless expander of social consciousness. In the early

eighties, before it was known exactly how AIDS was spread — before safer sex — I was catapulted into a panicked loss of a principle means of self-expression and contact with other humans. Now fucking casually meant more than a flouting of middle class standards and a mockery of middle class hygiene. It meant illness and death — deterioration.

In the first years of the AIDS crisis, my libidinal energy was turned inward and converted into obsessive self-examination of body and mind — as if I were look-ing for proof within of Nordau's degeneration. Being part of the AIDS risk group made me feel unclean, expendable, and marginalized, but I had no vehicle, no vibrant counterculture medium in which to express and share this. As is evident from contemporary rhetoric from the Right, the AIDS paradigm can be easily shaped to fit Nordau's theories. He would have seen it as a sick-ness of the body that can be traced to the sexual appetite of a degenerated brain, which is exactly how some on the Right speak of it today.

However, on the Left, AIDS became part of other strategies. Ironic as it may seem, it was a powerful force in mainstreaming homosexuality. Families who would never have known that a member was gay were forced to confront homosexuality with tragic acceptance when a son or brother became ill. The liberal mind was bom-barded with detailed descriptions of homosexual behav-ior by the medical profession and the media.

The mainstreaming of homosexuality was pushed along further by the new breed of activists. In fact, AIDS activism was to prove to be the only salient and effective radical political movement of the eighties. National awareness about AIDS, women's special health care needs, teenage sex, and sex education were all brought to the forefront of popular cultural discourse by AIDS activism, which at the time may have seemed strident or unrealistic but actually did result in influencing the big pharmaceutical companies, government health programs, public education, and the FDA.

The new activists of the epidemic, specifically those of ACT-UP, were even more firmly entrenched in a particular class reality than the people of the sixties counterculture had been. ACT-UP's members were mostly white and highly educated, and sometimes linked to insiders in advertising and the media. Despite ACT-UP's nonauthoritarian structure, some of its demonstrations were highly organized media events, which made ingenious use of fax machines, sophisticated graphics, and articulate speakers. However, I believe that the class orientation of most of the participants kept the AIDS movement from achieving more than a narrow focus. As women's issues, prison issues, race issues, and class issues came forward, the movement was fragmented and weakened.

AIDS escalated the absorption of homosexuality — at least temporarily — into the culture at large. But it left the true gay radical, the gay bohemian who harkened back to the gay separatist past, more alone than ever before. The old-style gay bohemian resented the media, was intrigued by other class realities, and scorned intimacy with the mainstream. If he became HIV positive, the kind of psychological support offered him by the AIDS establishment was likely to be repugnant to his values in some aspects. If he were negative, he found himself in the guilt-ridden position of feeling critical and contemptuous of such support.

When libido and experimentation have been curtailed within one subculture, the unrepentant bohemian may look elsewhere for energy. Those well-off radicals who rubbed shoulders with the working class in the thirties made their "descent" partly because they craved the simple, honest energy of hunger and anger— the energies of the culture of poverty. I found the objective correlative of my AIDS panic, self-doubt, and despair in the underclass culture documented by Oscar Lewis.

It began when the painter Scott Neary loaned me the 1983 novel *Saul's Book* by Paul T. Rogers. According to the short bio in the Penguin edition, the author of this first novel had been a schoolteacher and social worker; but after he was murdered by the Times Square hustler whom he had adopted and to whom he had dedicated *Saul's Book*, a cover article in the *Village Voice* revealed that Paul T. Rogers was very much like his character "Saul." He was a highly intelligent ex-con with one foot still in the embezzling underworld and an alcoholic and drug addict who frequented young hustlers.

Saul's Book is a pre-AIDS novel about the street life and street mind of a Times Square Puerto Rican hustler and heroin addict named Sinbad and his ongoing relationship with his Jewish trick, lover, and father figure Saul. In Sinbad, I sensed a much more vital and courageous version of my own despair about AIDS and lost identity. Making use of the skills of spontaneity, forgetfulness, impulsiveness, and casual generosity that Oscar Lewis detailed in *La Vida*, Sinbad manages to clothe his risk-filled life with the same flamboyant affectations and makeshift solutions that enraged Nordau and thrilled Mailer. As an underclass person he is, *de facto*, a person at risk. But instead of anguishing over his situation as I anguished in the mirror over blemishes, certain that they foretold illness and death, Sinbad launches into his sea of risk-filled pleasure with great elan and little self-preservation. In a perverse way he symbolized all the courage in extremity that I lacked. In the age of AIDS I went on a voyage to find the world of Sinbad, hoping to recover that sense of the old "degeneration" that had once linked underclass energies with the underground avant-garde.

Saul's Book helped transform me from a fearful and demoralized person who dabbled in writing into a driven writer on the way to becoming a novelist. A feeling of solidarity with the street people of Times Square whom I began to frequent gave me a way of incorporating my sense of being AIDS-endangered and expendable into an exciting literary endeavor. It also revived my hope of escaping the prison of my class and envisioning a new kind of counterculture. From then on, virtually all my writing was about the subject of underclass energy and the social comedy that is played out when middle class people in search of that energy come in contact with it as voyeurs, reformers, pleasure-seekers, or victims.

Little by little I began to realize that the malaise I had experienced before the AIDS crisis was due to the fact that bourgeois experience, encompassing my old homosexual identity, had been overcharted and was now laid out as neatly as the parking places at a strip mall. Beyond it was the unknown territory of the sexualized, drug-ridden street. Whereas Mailer had relied upon the medium of jazz and marijuana to bridge a gap between the paucity of his own middle class background and the exciting world of the street, I began to rely upon the only path of exchange left between the middle class and the underclass: prostitution and harder drugs.

I began hanging out in Times Square bars in 1984. By 1987 I was a familiar face in the neighborhood. I frequented male prostitutes, struck up love affairs with ex-cons, financially supported a throwaway child who eventually went to a drug treatment program, and experimented with drugs myself. I'm not boasting about what may appear to resemble a descent, nor am I recommending it to those trying to confront their own fear and trembling. It is merely something that happened at a moment in my life when all seemed hopeless and likely to end in catastrophe.

My descent galvanized my writing as if I had been given private access to a secret and infinite cosmos. Times Square mentalities charged my texts with a raw sexual ambiance that flirted with death. My identification with the people of the street allowed me to immerse myself in monologues that I could imagine taking place in their voices and their mind frame.

In his book, *Erotism*, Georges Bataille writes that "only the anti-social underworld preserves a quantity of energy that does not go into work." Bataille also claimed that the compensation for the humdrum of daily life was provided in pre-democratic days by the obscenely excit-

ing spectacle of royal privilege and in modern times by
the spectacle of the wealthy European playboy or
American gangster. This may be true, but in America
there are few representations of criminal excess that do
not rely upon the judgments of the police blotter or at
least the sentimentality of the kitchen-sink drama. *Last
Exit to Brooklyn* by Hubert Selby, Jr. is one of the beauti-
ful exceptions. *Manchild in a Promised Land* by Claude
Brown is another. The black exploitation novels of
Iceberg Slim and Donald Goines are even better exam-
ples. However, in most cases, when the underworld is
represented, the commercial exploitation of crime or
weepy ethnic nostalgia vampirizes all of the libido, energy, and aggression of Mailer's treasured "psychopaths"
and attaches the hypocritical disclaimer of a moral message at the end. For those thinkers and artists seriously
interested in the energies of the street, there are only three
possible approaches: one is the sober documentation and
analysis of underclass reality in the mind of a scientist,
like Oscar Lewis; another necessitates being born into
these realities as were Claude Brown and Hubert Selby,
Jr., and then miraculously pulling oneself up long enough
to conceptualize degradation with honesty and rage; or,
lastly, one can participate in these realities as an outsider,
situating oneself somewhere between voyeur and victim.

As a middle class person who wanted something
from the street, I found that the more prudent and self-
preserving I was, the more I became a voyeur, and the
less emotionally valid my connection to, my enjoyment
of, and consequently my writing about, this world. On the
other hand, the more I participated and the more risks I

took, the more libidinous and meaningful my connection to the world and my writing about it became.

However, participating in this world made it less likely that I would continue to write, as it entailed a heavy involvement in drugs, sex, risky ephemeral relationships, and petty criminal pursuits. I had to strike a very shaky balance between the stances of voyeur and participant to remain productive, which is not to say that I began to frequent Times Square for the purpose of writing a book. It was for the purpose of pleasure and because of despair that I found myself night after night in the company of junkies, crackheads, hustlers, and drag queen prostitutes. Even so, as I began to write a novel about my experiences, which was eventually published under the title *User*, my role stabilized, and I became part voyeur, part exploiter, part chronicler, and part victim.

I didn't realize until later that the Times Square of those years was the perfect milieu for someone like me. It was then (but because of gentrification and Disney's new investments in property will no longer be) the last crossroads of the classes in the old sense of "downtown," a central market place and neutral terrain where exchanges took place. Many of the people who came to buy drugs or sex in Times Square would not have dared to venture into the neighborhoods where those who sold these commodities lived. But in Times Square they had momentary, curtailed contact with these people, and I witnessed some of the old miracles of promiscuity and class mixes that I had valued in the past again taking place. Accordingly, when a hustler was arrested, and I went to Rikers' Island to post bail, the most surprising additional "friends" showed up; for top designers, champion prize fighters, devoted husbands with children, and politicians were also part-time frequenters of this world.

It took me four years to collect my notes and get into the right frame of mind to write *User*. I took my notes *in media res*, scribbling them on matchbook covers or napkins near the doors of the toilets in bars as crack smokers paraded in and out; at the bar counter, where fights sometimes erupted; sitting naked on the edge of beds in a pay-by-the hour hotel, after a trick had left; in after-hours clubs at dawn, where stoned queens and hustlers battled or made love; or on street corners, where I was sure to be hit up for one- and five-dollar bills by my so-called pals. This world of transactions was, in a perverse way, a fitting context for an exile from a counterculture that had distinguished itself by consumerism. However, here the players of the money game were the insiders, who belonged to "the Life" and the outsiders in search of pleasure, who served as their "marks," or victims, and were fleeced before ever being offered tangible goods.

In a world where aggression was only tensely leashed and private property depended upon who could get his hands on it, I discovered a surprising warmth and courage in the regulars. The street hood may be a loose cannon with rage and violence pulsing close to the surface, but his easy release of aggression leaves behind a kind of sweetness and generosity that the tight-assed bourgeois, full of pleasantries and buried resentments, never achieves. At the beginning, it amazed me when those bed partners who radiated a childlike warmth began to trust me enough to confess the violent crimes for which they'd done time. Suddenly the vigor of their sexual caresses titillated with other, frightening meanings, an ambiguity that they used to boost their moments of mastery over me, an exotic in their world. Likewise these people's early familiarity with physical pain, disappointment, and public institutions gave them the patience of fatalistic philosophers who could stomach rough treatment from medical personnel, suspicious behavior from sullen merchants, or long hours on bureaucratic lines that would drive most of us to distraction. It was clear that the muscular bodies they positioned within these many demeaning or risky social sites — welfare lines, police line-ups, drug-dealing corners — were their sole asset, radiating great vitality and nervous pride. But there was a crushing irony between these bodies and the map of abuse drawn on them by the many scars and bruises. They were like vital, valuable goods that had been mishandled. Their statuesque brutality, liquid eyes, and exhibitionistic stances intrigued me more than the carefully conditioned and cleaned bodies of my own class.

Politics was virtually nonexistent on the street. But in prison, which I visited quite often as one favorite after another was rounded up by the police, politics was startlingly radical and alienated. I remember going to Fishkill Correctional Facility several times to visit a twenty-seven-year-old of Puerto Rican background whom I'd meant by correspondence through another friend who was incarcerated. The twenty-seven-year-old had had a childhood of family violence and had been in prison for most of his adult life. Now he was often plagued by vicious nightmares of torture and witchcraft. Through courses in prison, he'd developed a high level of articulateness and was interested in revolutionary politics. This was during the Gulf War. He and his fellow inmates all supported Hussein. When I asked him why, he answered, "What has this country ever done for us?"

Through him and other inmates I learned about the Five Percenters, a politicized religious group developed and propagated in prisons during the seventies as one way of promoting Islamic culture. The name was based on the assertion that eighty-five percent of humanity are poor and uneducated and exploited by a controlling ten percent. The remaining five percent, who are the Five Percenters, claim to be exempt from exploitation because of their spiritual knowledge and emotional strength. At a time when complacent materialists were jumping on the Reagan band wagon, I found the loopy politics of my prison radical friends, whether reasonable or not, strangely refreshing.

Many who come from the culture of poverty and the street have stretched the boundaries of sexual identity in ways uninterpretable by middle class liberationist paradigms. My twenty-seven-year-old prison friend was straight-identified and always asked me for copies of *Penthouse*; but during collect calls and in letters, he took the homosexual tease to so graphic an extent that the most liberated proponents of male middle class consciousness-raising would be astonished or appalled. This was his way of paying me back with erotic stimulation for the books, clothing, or money I sent him. It was, of course, a form of commerce. But why did he have such a sure intuition for what could arouse me?

Bisexuality in prison, on the street, and throughout much of the Third World does not resemble that careful and philosophical bisexuality of our contemporary post-feminist, post-Freudian enlightenment. The street macho can be intensely homophobic and homosexual at the same time. The mixture of libido and flamboyant ego that spills out of the underclass male, as well as his familiarity with the skills of prostitution, make him available to both sexes in many instances. It's the role he plays that matters, regardless of which sex he does it with. The conditions of the culture of poverty — early sexual initiation, parents with multiple partners, and overcrowded living conditions in which siblings share the same bed in the same room as their elders — create a polymorphous sexuality that mocks our reductive categories of sexual identity. Although homosexuality may be vilified in macho settings, everyone knows that this is a policy for the surface and that many of the participants also have developed fully articulated same-sex sidelines, partly for survival and subsequently for pleasure. In the Anglo-Saxon world, with its heritage of philosophical materialism, the surface claims an exact match with what goes on underneath. But not so in the culture of poverty, where the bravado of appearances is one thing and off-the-record experiences and feelings are another. A man's got to have an image but he must not become a slave to it.

The sophisticated interplay between surface realities and inner realities in underclass life is in sharp contrast to the reductive tendencies of class-prejudiced identity politics, with its formula of actions equaling identity. And the controversies of the closet and outing — two favorites of gay politics — collapse into superficiality in the context of the street. In Times Square I met many married men who were not homosexual but who had a passion for transvestites. Sometimes they even enjoyed being the passive partner with someone who had both a penis and a female image (breasts, etc.). But they would have been repulsed by the idea of having sex with anyone who looked like a man. They simply were not gay.

A hustler I knew did it less for the money than for isolated heightened experiences in which he could lose himself sucking cock while he focused on a straight porno film playing in the background. During these fugue states, I could sense his fantasies flow in shifting, disembodied identifications with the man in the film, then the woman, then with me, and then with himself as someone with a cock in his mouth. He was intensely attracted to women and had a wife but was probably capable of a whole pattern of relationships with males on a deeply felt level. Still, he preferred to accumulate homosexual feelings until they spilled out in isolated erotic episodes. If he'd been "outed" — if he'd been forced to articulate all the libido he'd accumulated around the ritualistic episodes of cock-sucking into something rational and community-minded — he probably would have lost his complicated erotic relationships with the women and men in his life. There are sexual impulses which are too fragmented to base an entire sociological identity upon. To brand them simply as "closeted" is intolerant and presumptuous.

If one must find identity in homosexuality, then all that really remains are some disturbing physical and social factors: Homosexuals can't make babies with each other, and nonproduction of a family automatically sets one outside the mainstream. In his erotic activity, the homosexual is likely to encounter other outsiders, such as bisexuals. In a country that functions upon the assumptions of fixed identities, bisexuals are likely to lead unconventional lives that partake of other marginalized populations. For example, there is a heavy incidence of bisexuality in the world of drug users and in the culture of poverty. This means that the homosexual, who will encounter bisexuals, is likely to be interfaced occasionally with these populations at risk. Because of its nonbreeding status and its association with marginality, homosexuality is one ideal position from which to challenge the conventional structures of society. It could again serve as the starting point for a new class-oriented counterculture mentality.

Today, identity politics is one of many facets of the middle class mentality that has absorbed some marginals and worked to sever the old, fertile connections between bohemia, the culture of poverty, and the avant-garde. Such politics spends a lot of time fearfully discussing the uncontrollability of libidinal behavior and deconstructing aestheticism while it continues to neglect the embarrassing subject of class. Concurrently, it has become the voice of one ruling class — the homogenized suburban bourgeoisie. For the liberal, there are many ironies in the new politics; among them is the following: about those we liberals have been taught not to vilify — the poor — there is now no language to speak about at all.

Lack of class consciousness is America's glaring, unspoken sin. There has been no voice to discuss class since the thirties, when the working class was at stake and before America became a service economy. Whether a particular voice of today's "multiculturism" has a black face, a woman's face, a gay face, or a working class background is now besides the point. All speak the language of the well-fed.

The denaturing of class issues was helped along by deconstructionist specialists in the universities, who dismantled politically offensive canonical texts and approved of or condemned behavior without anthropolog- ical reference to the intrinsic values of the people from which it sprang. The devaluation of some of the more sociologically authentic, sensual, deranged, and aesthetic literary texts we have began with the aim of liberation from imposed norms and ended up by boilerplating the burgeoning id, which is by definition obscene and aggressive, but which is the fount of energy for the creative artist. When it comes to discussing outsider culture, academics have invented distanced cynical terms like "performance" or "transgression." Giving voice to the reality of poverty in all its lustiness, energy, and degradation has become taboo, and it is actually considered a slight to a poor person's integrity to tell the reality of his cultural experiences.

For the gelded inhabitant of today's so-called counterculture, I see only one possible action in the face of a voiceless, unacknowledged underclass and a strangulated middle class. That is a mental coalition between the disaffected bohemian and the culture of poverty. Street people speak of appetites and aggressions that artistic middle class people can help them articulate. But first it must be admitted that in underclass life, identity cannot be conveniently sifted out and defined. Hunger, homelessness, or drug addiction always take precedence. On the street, everybody is a "nigger." And there is a certain depth of need or disorganization at which a person will stick it in anybody or let anyone at all stick it in.

These chaotic energies are the "sickness" that Nordau thought the avant-garde artists of his time had been infected with. And it was from this swamp of urban libido that some of our century's richest artistic creations were to flower. The same alchemy is possible in the next century, but more so, for never before has the dichotomy of middle class decency and urban degeneration been more skewed.

EPILOGUE

ON LOSING TIMES SQUARE

As a writer I've found myself attracted to alienated consciousnesses — people trapped for better or worse in the margins. They seem to provide the originality, the libido, and the drive to make me generate "imaginative" prose. Consequently, my summer reading is more likely to resemble *Last Exit to Brooklyn* than *Rabbit Run*. But in frequent intervals the desktop seems barren, so I give it the slip and disappear into Times Square. In this world, I profit from the excitement of dangerous underclass energies, from which my first-generation-immigrant parents, struggling for security, spent a lifetime protecting me. I come home contaminated with inspiration, then sleep it off until the afternoon.

After years of hanging out in Times Square, I'm a familiar figure. Occasionally, I am still walking the streets as the sky melts into dawn. But no matter how long I stay, I will never be able to capture what is rapidly being drained from this neighborhood. Times Square is being transformed from a place of illicit pleasure transactions into a prefabricated theme park for the family.

What Times Square is losing can be found nowhere else. Up until this moment it had been a place where "the underworld meets the elite," where those who have no cash encountered those who have a little or a lot. It was here that people who could afford $60 seats at Broadway shows faced the young and the poor coming for the video arcades and budget double features. Times Square was a crossroads of class and race. It was one of the only places where the burned-out South Bronx could touch boutiqued-out Manhattan.

At this date, all but a few of the original buildings of Times Square's major thoroughfare, 42nd Street, which has been purchased by the state, are boarded up. The porno shops have been shunted to Eighth Avenue, where they bide their time until a new city ban against sexually explicit material may eliminate all but a few. As if an army of children could complete the transformation from Red Light district into Souvenir City, a children's theater called the Victory has taken the lead on the block. It was the first finished renovation; then Disney opened its superstore across the street and is now working on its heavily subsidized renovation of the New Amsterdam Theater. A few blocks away on Broadway, the new Virgin megastore rules, next to a smug and plastic All-Star Cafe, a sports-theme restaurant. Sentimental nonauthenticity, which is the genius of suburbia, has taken the lead in Times Square. It is epitomized by the new establishments' use of vacuum-molded plastic-and-steel facsimiles of art deco trim, which serves as a cynical tip of the hat to Times Square's architectural past. What used to be sordid is being replaced by pseudo.

During my Times Square vigils of several years ago, I followed a fairly set itinerary that began with a happy hour drink at a hustler bar, moved on to a bar that was a Manhattan hangout for the Latin Kings, took in a Blarney Stone favored by gay blacks, sampled a drag club called La Fiesta, and ended up a little further east in the 40s at an after-hours club in a building that still had the original interior staircase from the time it was a private home.

Today, I still drop in at another long-standing club called Sally's II, which is one of the last old-style drag bars in Manhattan. It's a place where dressed-to-the-tits queens, most of them Latin or Black, saunter past sulky homeboys in their oversized jeans. Lustful businessmen in black suits still carrying their attaché cases — who remind you of somebody's father — hug tumblers of bourbon, scoping out the "female" trade. Even today, clients remain caught up in the fast action — that steamy tango of opposites that makes the bars of old Times Square so vital and so threatening.

Last night, as on most nights, the staff rounded out the homage to heteroland. Two tough daddy-bouncers ruled with an iron hand, while big-breasted queens bitch-nurtured, serving drinks. The air was thick with *familia*. Everybody knew everybody else's name, and all knew me as "the guy who writes those books about us," though few had read them.

The legendary Sally who started the club succumbed to AIDS several years ago. Sometimes he showed up in female drag for special occasions, such as his birthday, but emceed most of the shows in Vegas-male drag, lip-synching Sinatra or Tom Jones.

Sally's II is undeniably urban, but is also a village. It's a tightly knit community of people with complementary needs yet different economic, ethnic, and cultural backgrounds. From the first I was struck by how little it resembles a "gay bar" in today's mainstream sense of the word. Its careful simulations of guys and dolls has a peculiar symbiotic relationship to the normal, straight world.

Not far from Sally's was the dungeon of a friend of mine, a sophisticated house of dominatrices who catered to the sadomasochistic impulses of rich gentlemen. Occasionally, I'd stop up and have a drink in the office with my friend, while the muffled sounds of slaps or groans came from the adjoining rooms.

The only thing that connected this world of expensive pleasure transactions to the bars I visited was the reliance of both upon the commerce of pleasure, but Times Square was big enough to accommodate each of them. Now, all but one of my bars has been closed. Sally's II has been harassed several times by a suddenly vigilant police department. My friend was pressured out of her dungeon by the Department of Housing Preservation and Development, along with artists who had occupied the other floors of the building for years.

But even today, I still see cars from suburban New Jersey barreling to the curb to pick up drugs being sold by somebody from the ghetto of East New York. I still catch glimpses of the businessmen from Connecticut stiffly walking a female or transvestite prostitute to a pay-by-the-hour hotel. And I can still find working class Blarney Stone bars serving cheap drinks to construction workers, janitors, tourists from Germany, yuppies, and the homeless.

Times Square is still a tense node of the uneasy American scene. Its crown — the great building of the Port Authority Bus Terminal — still serves as a squalid Notre Dame for the homeless as well as a pipeline for millions of middle class commuters and tourists. The neighborhood is a leftover of the old center-city notion

— known in most metropolitan areas as "downtown." And those mornings after I have squandered the night, as squeamish commuters thread through the leftovers, I mourn the vanishing of such a site.

"Downtown" is certainly not a recent phenomenon. The central marketplace, where the poor and the rich were forced to have contact for the sake of business and pleasure, goes back to ancient times. But in fitting with the new millennium of sprawl, the days of the intense city center are numbered. Many applaud this "clean-up." But these are the people who do not object to the uniform visuals of today's malls, who never question dependence on the automobile, and who lead a life style that is only in theory multicultural. Ironically, they are also the people who consume products that depend in part on the energies of the rejected classes, since fashion designers, musicians, and advertisers vandalize the physicality and dynamism of the poor to package libido for consumers. They have made use of tropical colors, African music, "exterminator" spices, and the passionate fatality of boxing, while the originators of these energies continue to press their noses to the opposite side of the glass, yearningly fixated on the washed-out elegance of a Virginia Slims girl or an accessorized *GQ* man.

As I wallow in my waning degenerate center-city paradise, I reflect on the ways that the terrain of the Other is shrinking in America. To me, suburban America seems omnipresent. Times Square is not the only neighborhood in Manhattan being swallowed up by the new blandness. When Manhattan became one of the last urban centers to alter zoning laws to allow the opening of more and more large convenience stores, the new chains became way stations for the promotion of uniform values, icons of nuclear family politics that multiplied like clones. These value stations came from the minds of people who would rather risk danger from machines (car accidents) than from people (muggings); but because of them, the very notion of travel may now become obsolete. Each store is identical to the next, making it soon feasible to shop with friends via video in two different outlets of Staples or catch dinner with a mother living in another town at a communal cyberspace Red Lobster.

I am well aware of the perversity of my reasoning. Yet as I track the giving way to progress in old Times Square, I can't help but remember it in the seventies and eighties as a bustling center of cheap movie houses and video arcades, where mostly nonwhite, low-income people took their dates, seemingly oblivious to the porno palaces next door. And I wonder where these people spend Saturday nights now. Contact — however brief — outside the prison of my class is what I still desire. Then call me, if you will, a degenerate, and look for me "Downtown."

READINGS

Bataille, Georges. *Erotism: Death and Sensuality*. San Francisco: City Lights, 1986.

Benderson, Bruce. *User*. New York: Dutton/Plume, 1994.

Goines, Donald. *Dope Fiend*. Los Angeles: Holloway House, 1971, 1991.

Lewis, Oscar. *La Vida: A Puerto Rican Family in the Culture of Poverty*. New York: Random House, 1966.

Mailer, Norman. *The White Negro*. San Francisco: City Lights, 1957.

Nordau, Max. *Degeneration*. Translated from the second edition of the German work (original publication: 1895). Introduction by George L. Mosse. Lincoln, Nebraska: University of Nebraska Press, 1993.

Rogers, Paul T. *Saul's Book*. New York: Pushcart Press, 1983, and New York: Penguin Books, 1983, 1984.

Slim, Iceberg. *Long White Con*. Los Angeles: Holloway House, 1977.

Sukenick, Ronald. *Down and In: Life in the Underground*. New York: Collier Books, 1989.